D1192966

BY ALLAN MOREY

THE LOS ANGELES
RAMS
STORY

BELLWETHER MEDIA · MINNEAPOLIS, MN

™

Are you ready to take it to the extreme? Torque books thrust you into the action-packed world of sports, vehicles, mystery, and adventure. These books may include dirt, smoke, fire, and chilling tales. **WARNING** : read at your own risk.

This edition first published in 2017 by Bellwether Media, Inc.

No part of this publication may be reproduced in whole or in part without written permission of the publisher. For information regarding permission, write to Bellwether Media, Inc., Attention: Permissions Department, 5357 Penn Avenue South, Minneapolis, MN 55419.

Library of Congress Cataloging-in-Publication Data

Names: Morey, Allan, author.
Title: The Los Angeles Rams Story / by Allan Morey.
Description: Minneapolis, MN : Bellwether Media, Inc., 2017. | Series:
    Torque: NFL Teams | Includes bibliographical references and index.
Identifiers: LCCN 2015037209 | ISBN 9781626173835 (hardcover : alk. paper)
Subjects: LCSH: St. Louis Rams (Football team)–History–Juvenile literature.
Classification: LCC GV956.S85 M67 2017 | DDC 796.332/640977866–dc23
LC record available at http://lccn.loc.gov/2015037209

Printed in the United States of America, North Mankato, MN.

TABLE OF CONTENTS

It is December 27, 2015. The Rams are in Seattle, Washington. They face the Seahawks, one of the best teams in the National Football League (NFL).

Tavon Austin

Akeem Ayers

Early in the game, Rams linebacker Akeem Ayers picks up a fumble. He runs the ball 45 yards into the end zone. Touchdown!

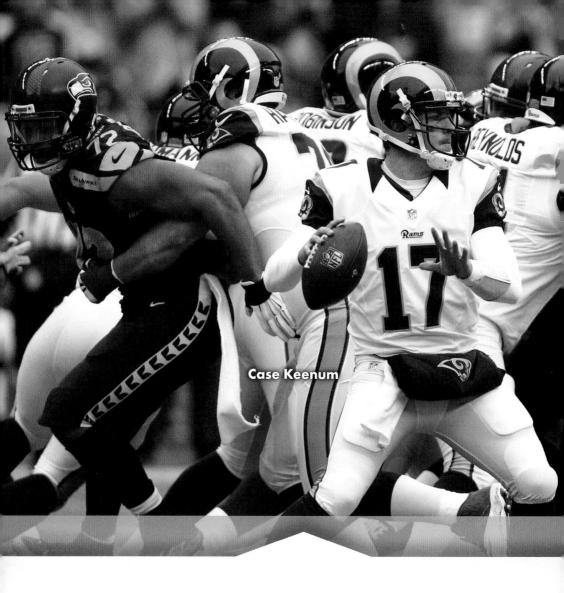

Case Keenum

The Seahawks only score one field goal in the first half. The Rams lead 16 to 3 at halftime.

In the second half, the Seahawks score two touchdowns. But the Rams also score one. They go on to win 23 to 17. It is their last win as a St. Louis team.

SCORING TERMS

END ZONE

the area at each end of a football field; a team scores by entering the opponent's end zone with the football.

EXTRA POINT

a score that occurs when a kicker kicks the ball between the opponent's goal posts after a touchdown is scored; 1 point.

FIELD GOAL

a score that occurs when a kicker kicks the ball between the opponent's goal posts; 3 points.

SAFETY

a score that occurs when a player on offense is tackled behind his own goal line; 2 points for defense.

TOUCHDOWN

a score that occurs when a team crosses into its opponent's end zone with the football; 6 points.

TWO-POINT CONVERSION

a score that occurs when a team crosses into its opponent's end zone with the football after scoring a touchdown; 2 points.

SUPER BOWL 34
JANUARY 30, 2000

The Rams were once called "The Greatest Show on Turf." From 1999 to 2001, their explosive offense scored a ton of points. Quarterback Kurt Warner was slinging touchdowns.

SUPER BOWL WINNERS
In 2000, The Greatest Show on Turf won Super Bowl 34. In that game, Warner threw touchdown passes to both Bruce and Holt.

His favorite targets were wide receivers Isaac Bruce and Torry Holt. On the ground, running back Marshall Faulk was punching the ball into the end zone.

LOS ANGELES
MEMORIAL COLISEUM

Three different cities have been the Rams' home. The team formed in Cleveland, Ohio. Then the Rams moved to Los Angeles, California, and later to St. Louis, Missouri. In each city, the Rams secured a league championship.

As of 2016, the Rams are back in California at the Los Angeles Memorial **Coliseum**.

11

The Rams joined the NFL in 1937. Today, they play in the National Football **Conference** (NFC). They are in the West **Division**.

The West Division includes the Seattle Seahawks, San Francisco 49ers, and Arizona Cardinals. It is a tough division. Both the Seahawks and 49ers have made it to the **Super Bowl** recently.

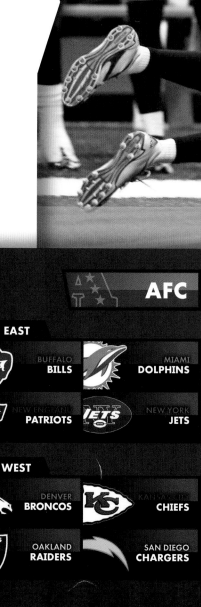

NFL DIVISIONS

AFC

AFC NORTH

 BALTIMORE **RAVENS**

CINCINNATI **BENGALS**

CLEVELAND **BROWNS**

PITTSBURGH **STEELERS**

AFC EAST

BUFFALO **BILLS**

MIAMI **DOLPHINS**

NEW ENGLAND **PATRIOTS**

NEW YORK **JETS**

AFC SOUTH

HOUSTON **TEXANS**

INDIANAPOLIS **COLTS**

 JACKSONVILLE **JAGUARS**

TENNESSEE **TITANS**

AFC WEST

DENVER **BRONCOS**

KANSAS CITY **CHIEFS**

 RAIDERS OAKLAND **RAIDERS**

SAN DIEGO **CHARGERS**

NFC

NFC **NORTH**

 CHICAGO
BEARS

 DETROIT
LIONS

 GREEN BAY
PACKERS

 MINNESOTA
VIKINGS

NFC **EAST**

 DALLAS
COWBOYS

 NEW YORK
GIANTS

 PHILADELPHIA
EAGLES

 WASHINGTON
REDSKINS

NFC **SOUTH**

 ATLANTA
FALCONS

 CAROLINA
PANTHERS

 NEW ORLEANS
SAINTS

TAMPA BAY
BUCCANEERS

NFC **WEST**

 ARIZONA
CARDINALS

 LOS ANGELES
RAMS

 SAN FRANCISCO
49ERS

 SEATTLE
SEAHAWKS

The Rams got off to a slow start in Cleveland. The team's first winning season did not come until 1945. But they won the NFL Championship that year!

The next year, the Rams moved to Los Angeles. They continued their winning ways in their new home. They were NFL champions again in 1951.

NFL CHAMPIONSHIP
DECEMBER 23, 1951

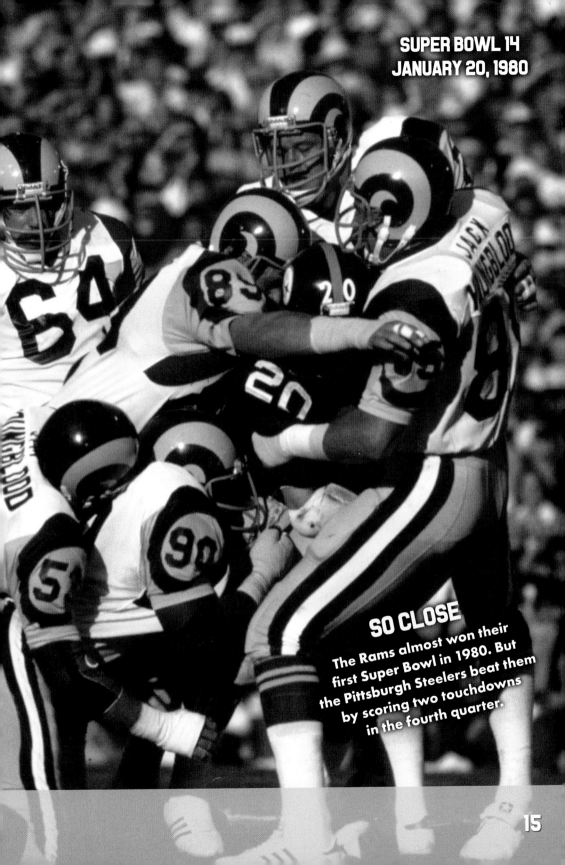

SO CLOSE

The Rams almost won their first Super Bowl in 1980. But the Pittsburgh Steelers beat them by scoring two touchdowns in the fourth quarter.

In 1995, the Rams moved to St. Louis. A few years later, Warner joined the team as quarterback. As leader of The Greatest Show on Turf, he took the Rams to two Super Bowls.

Kurt Warner

Kenny Britt

The Rams have struggled lately. But L.A. fans are happy to have the team back. The team is focused on making the **playoffs** again!

RAMS TIMELINE

1945

Won their first NFL Championship, beating the Washington Redskins

15 FINAL SCORE **14**

1937

Joined the NFL

1946

Moved to Los Angeles, California

1951

Won their second NFL Championship, beating the Cleveland Browns (24-17)

2000

Won Super Bowl 34, beating the Tennessee Titans

23 FINAL SCORE **16**

1998

Welcomed star quarterback Kurt Warner to the team

1995

Moved to St. Louis, Missouri

1999

Welcomed star running back Marshall Faulk to the team

2016

Moved back to Los Angeles, California

In the 1960s, the Rams had the "Fearsome Foursome." Hall-of-Famers David "Deacon" Jones and Merlin Olsen were half of this all-star **defensive line**.

Merlin Olsen

David "Deacon" Jones

SAID IT FIRST
"Sacking the quarterback" is a phrase started by Jones.

Eric Dickerson

Eric Dickerson ran onto the scene in the 1980s. In 1984, he rushed for 2,105 yards. This still stands as the NFL's single-season rushing record!

21

During the St. Louis years, Warner went from being a backup quarterback to a Super Bowl Most Valuable Player (MVP). Faulk was a star from the start. In each of his first three years as a Ram, he was named the NFL's Offensive Player of the Year.

Today, running back Todd Gurley is an offensive force. As a rookie, he rushed for more than 1,100 yards.

TEAM GREATS

DAVID "DEACON" JONES
DEFENSIVE END
1961-1971

ERIC DICKERSON
RUNNING BACK
1983-1987

ISAAC BRUCE
WIDE RECEIVER
1994-2007

Todd Gurley

KURT WARNER
QUARTERBACK
1998-2003

MARSHALL FAULK
RUNNING BACK
1999-2005

TORRY HOLT
WIDE RECEIVER
1999-2008

The Rams have long been NFL trailblazers. For many years, football players wore solid-colored helmets. But in 1948, the Rams painted horns on theirs. Now most teams decorate their helmets, too.

Then in 1950, the Rams thrilled home audiences. They were the first team to show all their games on TV.

In 2016, the Rams brought **professional** football back to the second-largest city in the United States. Los Angeles fans have celebrated the return.

Rampage

Los Angeles stadium plans

A new stadium is being built for almost $3 billion. And Rampage, the team mascot, now has a star on Hollywood's Walk of Fame!

MORE ABOUT THE
RAMS

Team name:
Los Angeles Rams

Team name explained:
Named after New York's
Fordham University Rams

Nicknames:
The Greatest Show on Turf,
Fearsome Foursome

Joined NFL: 1937

Conference: NFC

Division: West

**Main rivals: San Francisco 49ers,
Seattle Seahawks**

Hometown:
Los Angeles, California

Training camp location:
River Ridge Fields, Oxnard, California

CALIFORNIA

LOS ANGELES ———————○

Home stadium name: Los Angeles Memorial Coliseum

Stadium opened: 1923

Seats in stadium: 93,607

Logo: The head of a ram, or male sheep

Colors: Blue and gold

Mascot: Rampage

RAMPAGE

GLOSSARY

coliseum—a large arena

conference—a large grouping of sports teams that often play one another

defensive line—the players on defense who try to stop the quarterback; defensive linemen crouch down in front of the ball.

division—a small grouping of sports teams that often play one another; usually there are several divisions of teams in a conference.

fumble—a loose ball that is still in play

linebacker—a player on defense whose main job is to make tackles and stop passes; a linebacker stands just behind the defensive linemen.

offense—the group of players who try to move down the field and score

playoffs—the games played after the regular NFL season is over; playoff games determine which teams play in the Super Bowl.

professional—a player or team that makes money playing a sport

quarterback—a player on offense whose main job is to throw and hand off the ball

rookie—a first-year player in a sports league

running back—a player on offense whose main job is to run with the ball

rushed—ran with the ball

Super Bowl—the championship game for the NFL

trailblazers—people or groups of people who make or do something first

turf—the grasslike surface of a football field

wide receivers—players on offense whose main job is to catch passes from the quarterback

TO LEARN MORE

AT THE LIBRARY

Braun, Eric. *Super Bowl Records.* Mankato, Minn.: Capstone Press, 2016.

Graves, Will. *The Best NFL Offenses of All Time.* Minneapolis, Minn.: ABDO Publishing Company, 2014.

Labrecque, Ellen. *NFC West.* Mankato, Minn.: Child's World, 2012.

ON THE WEB

Learning more about the Los Angeles Rams is as easy as 1, 2, 3.

1. Go to www.factsurfer.com.

2. Enter "Los Angeles Rams" into the search box.

3. Click the "Surf" button and you will see a list of related web sites.

With factsurfer.com, finding more information is just a click away.

INDEX